PRAYERS AND LITURGIES OF CONFESSION AND ASSURANCE

Kenneth H. Carter Jr.

Abingdon Press
Nashville

JUST IN TIME!
PRAYERS AND LITURGIES OF CONFESSION AND ASSURANCE

Copyright © 2009 by Abingdon Press

This book is printed on acid-free paper.

Library of Congress Cataloging-in-Publication Data

Carter, Kenneth H.
   Prayers and liturgies of confession and assurance / Kenneth H. Carter, Jr.
      p. cm. — (Just in time!)
   Includes indexes.
   ISBN 978-0-687-65489-5 (binding: pbk., adhesive perfect : alk. paper)
   1. Confession (Liturgy)—Christianity. 2. Confession (Liturgy)—Texts. 3. Church year. I. Title.

BV845.C37 2009
264'.13—dc22

2008021163

09 10 11 12 13 14 15 16 17 18—10 9 8 7 6 5 4 3 2 1
MANUFACTURED IN THE UNITED STATES OF AMERICA

CONTENTS

Contents

Contents

INTRODUCTION

We practice ministry and gather as Christians in the midst of "worship wars." In the last century, the patterns and rituals of our worship were passed, uncontested for the most part, from generation to generation. And while warfare might be too strong a word to describe our conversations and debates about worship, particularly in a time of warfare around the globe, worship practices are no longer uncontested. This is true for styles of music, oral communication, the presence or absence of visual images, and the structure of the worship service itself.

There is a real question, in the midst of these debates, about the need for confession of sin within the service of Christian worship. Some see confession as a set of rote expressions, sometimes disconnected from human behavior. Others view confession as a "downer" in the midst of more upbeat praise experiences. Yet others view worship as the reconstruction of the self-esteem of the individual; confession is an unnecessary detour on that journey.

Some congregants have insisted to me that they do not feel that they have sinned; others do not quite see themselves in the words of confession. As a pastor I take these conversations very seriously. And yet, my reading of Scripture, my sense of the tradition, and my pastoral experience is heavily weighted in a different direction.

The reality of sin is deeply embedded in the biblical witness: from the first saga, of Adam and Eve, through the lineage of the patriarchs and matriarchs to the enslavement of Israel by Pharaoh—and that's just Genesis. Sin is pervasive throughout Scripture: from the social environment that called forth the rebuke of the prophets to the religious leaders who resisted the ministry of Jesus to the conflict and immorality that existed in early Christian communities.

The teaching of the Scriptures across the centuries in the church, especially in the context of worship, led to the need for a formal recognition of confession of sin, often as a response to having come into the presence of a God who is worthy of our praise and adoration. These confessions were sometimes corporate, sometimes offered by the priest on behalf of the church, and sometimes related to the liturgical calendar.

The tradition of confession serves God's people best when it is in conversation with the rich diversity of human experience: personal and structural sin (see Reinhold Niebuhr's classic *Moral Man and Immoral Society*), recurrent moral failure, remembrance of past horrors (as in the confession of complicity in racism or genocide), or attempts to discover meaning in human tragedy.

Biblical faith teaches us to hold in tension our need to confess sin with God's gracious offer of forgiveness. Without confession, we are not honest in examining our own lives before God or others in the human family. And yet confession itself, apart from assurance, leads to a demoralized condition and a downcast spirit. At the same time, assurance without confession (and repentance) results in "cheap grace." The pastor and the laity are also aware that all of God's people are in need of both confession and assurance; as the Apostle Paul wrote, "All have sinned and fall short of the glory of God" (Romans 3:23).

Please note that the liturgies are punctuated with intentional occasions for silence. View these moments as spaces for the Spirit of God to move in the minds and hearts of those in worship. Do not move too quickly from silence to word—our culture is prone to fill all time with activity and all pauses with words. Allow appropriate time—start with fifteen seconds, then, as participants grow more comfortable, thirty or forty-five seconds—for silence. God is present in the silence!

This brief volume begins with three meditations on sin: first, a reflection on the sin of *pride*, often noted as the first of the "seven deadly sins"; second, an examination of the Ten Commandments as *boundaries* given to us by God; and third, a discussion of *for-giveness* as our need, our witness, and our gospel.

Following these meditations are three chapters of liturgies, each including a prayer of confession and words of assurance. Each liturgy follows a similar format:

- A choral or congregational call to prayer. You will want to adapt the suggestion to your own worship setting.
- An invitation to silence and prayer.
- A time of silence, noted by a cross: "✝ *Silence*."
- A prayer of confession: offered by the leader, by the whole congregation, or adapted as responsive readings. A second time of silence, noted by the sign of the cross.
- Words of Assurance.

These suggestions are marked by attention to the human condition, to biblical sources, and to the liturgical year. Of course, some can be cross-referenced (e.g., Advent is a time of waiting; Lent is a time of testing). Some also include a suggested Scripture reading for context and preparation.

These are imperfect prayers. "We do not know how to pray as we ought," Paul writes in Romans 8:26. "We know in part," Paul writes elsewhere, in 1 Corinthians 13. There is more to say, and surely there is language that comes closer to the truth. I yearn for it; yet I am finite. And so I hope that God will accept these offerings, and that you, the reader, will benefit from them, saying these prayers in ways that lead you more fully into the awareness of your own human condition, and also into the grace of God.

CHAPTER ONE

REFLECTIONS ON SIN: WHY DO WE NEED TO CONFESS?

SIN AS PRIDE

Sin has been defined as the inner condition that exists when we are not who God wants us to be. Sin as an inner condition is a prominent theme in Scripture (e.g., Psalm 51 and Romans 7). This inner condition leads to external behaviors that are visible and tangible, but sin is the inner condition. It is relational. If there is no God, there is no sin.

Sin is prevalent, occasional, and predictable in human experience, and Christians have attempted to analyze it in a number of ways. Christians have talked about seven *deadly* sins for about sixteen hundred years. Seekers who wanted a closer relationship with Jesus would go out into the desert regions of Egypt and Syria, and would there examine themselves. These seven sins—pride, envy, anger, boredom, greed, gluttony, lust—were the ones with which many individuals struggled. They shape our struggles as well. These are the sins that destroy people. These are the sins that end relationships. These are the sins that damage families and friendships. These are the sins that corrupt businesses and communities. These are the sins that wreak havoc among the nations.

The first and most basic of these sins is *pride*. C. S. Lewis wrote of one vice of which no one in the world is free, which we all despise when we see it in other people, and which hardly any people—except Christians—ever imagine that they are guilty of. This is the sin of pride. Pride leads to every other sin. Lewis says, "It was through Pride that the devil became the devil" and that pride is "spiritual cancer" (*Mere Christianity* [San Francisco: HarperCollins, 2001], 122, 125). That should get our attention. Pride is the core sin; Lewis calls it the "great sin." I want to reflect on the sin of pride in very simple and straightforward ways.

"I thank you, God, that I'm not like *them*."

We confront pride when we hear or say the words "I'm better than other people." The religious man in the parable in Luke goes up to the temple to pray and says, "God, I thank you that I am not like other people. . . . I fast twice a week; I give a tenth of all my income" (Luke 18:11-12).

There is something to be said for this Pharisee. His relationship with God is shaping his life and his values to the extent that he has disciplined his spending of money to give one tenth (a tithe) to God. In addition he has disciplined his eating so that he doesn't just miss a meal or fast for a day; he fasts two days a week. He is obedient to God. He is righteous. But the sin of pride has entered his life. "I'm better than other people," he thinks. He even puts it in the form of a prayer: "I thank you, God, that I'm not like these other people."

One of my favorite spiritual guides is the author Flannery O'Connor. She was a native of Milledgeville, Georgia, and she died of lupus in the middle of life. O'Connor was a person of deep Christian faith. In one of her stories, "Revelation," a woman is sitting in a doctor's office talking about people (when we are at our worst, we sometimes talk about other people). This woman says to herself and to anyone who will listen, "I thank you God that you didn't make me and my husband Claude black. But if the choice was between making me black and making me white trash, God, I would rather you make me black. I couldn't bear to be white trash." And at about that time a young woman also in the waiting room whacks her over the head with a book. As a result of the impact she becomes dizzy and is carried off to the hospital. At the end of the story she has a dream, a revelation, that there is a great band of folk dancing their way up the ladder to heaven—prostitutes and thieves and blacks and white trash and there, at the end, are she and her husband Claude. (Read the full story in *The Complete Stories* [New York: Farrar, Straus and Giroux, 1972], 405-24.)

Jesus said, to the religious leaders of his day, "the tax collectors and the prostitutes are going into the kingdom of God ahead of you" (Matthew 21:31). When pride gets the best of us we think, "I'm better than other people."

I Don't Need God

In its ultimate form, pride can also mean "I don't need God." And when we have no God, we make a God of ourselves. When Christ is not at the center, we place ourselves at the center. Think about the life of a professional athlete. From childhood he (this pattern is most prevalent for males) is a star. People tell him that he is a star. He excels in high school and college, and before he ever plays a game in the pros he has made more money than all of his relatives and neighbors will make in their lifetimes.

His job as a professional athlete comes with many benefits, among them an instant group of "close" friends. A few years ago I spent the night in a hotel in a big city, and two professional sports teams were staying there. Because I'm tall, some might have mistaken me for one the team members, but I am no longer the age of pro athletes. Time passes by!

There were a lot of folks at that hotel who were only too ready to be friends with these athletes. The women were attractive; the men had connections or gifts. These hangers-on wanted a piece of the star athletes. In these cases, what the athlete gets in return is someone who will run errands, agree with almost anything he says, and get him anything he desires.

These relationships are all maintained at the discretion of the star. If he tires of the men, he ends the relationship—they do not. If he tires of a woman, he ends the relationship—she does not. It is a warped universe in which the star athlete is the center. Everything revolves around him. This is the sin of pride. It is as easy to follow as the evening news or the morning paper.

"Pride," Proverbs 16:18 says, "goes before destruction." Sometimes pride is obvious, but sometimes pride is subtle. The danger for us is to say, "I thank you, God, that I am not like a person who would act that way." Sometimes pride is obvious, but sometimes pride is more subtle.

I grew up in a medium-sized church in the Deep South. In that church I was taught the Bible, I was baptized, I was given opportunities to serve, and I sang in the choir. I was loved. In that church I answered a call to full-time ministry and went off to seminary.

A year into seminary, I was invited back to preach. Recently I came across that printed sermon in some old papers. It was truly awful. The spirit of the sermon was that I had come back from *on high* to share my wisdom with these people. I had been to seminary for a year and studied the New Testament in the original Greek for a whole year, and so now I knew everything and they knew nothing. I didn't say the words, but it was there, written between the lines—pride. On that Sunday long ago, I did not come to share the gospel. I came to display my pride. Even in the guise of preaching the gospel, pride entered into my life, and I swallowed it like a trout going for a fly in a mountain stream.

Overcoming Pride

How do we overcome this core sin of pride, which is sometimes obvious and sometimes subtle? We discover a change in attitude; a shift in perspective; a repentance of heart—humility. We overcome pride through humility. The Bible links these two words: *pride* and *humility*. "God opposes the proud," James 4:6 reminds us, "but gives grace to the humble."

In Luke's telling of the encounter between the Pharisee and the tax collector (18:9-14), we see both pride and humility. In the first century, Jews listening to a rabbi would do one of two things if something was said with which they disagreed: (1) if they were outside, they would throw sand into the air; (2) if they were inside, they would throw up their arms. Can you imagine what people would have done as they listened to the teaching of Jesus?

In this parable, Jesus says that two men are in the temple to pray, a religious leader and a tax collector. The fact that the tax collector was there is pretty amazing and would have been disturbing to anyone who heard this teaching. As we have already seen, the religious man has done everything right, all that is acceptable in the sight of God, but he is eaten up with pride. Jesus says that only one of the two men is in a right relationship with God: the tax collector. People would have waved their hands and objected.

Tax collectors may not be popular today, but in first-century Israel they were truly despised. The tax collector prays, "God, be merciful to me, a sinner." I call this prayer of seven words "the humility prayer." The humility prayer helps us overcome pride:

- As we say these seven words, we *confess our need*. We need help; we are sinners.
- As we say these seven words, we *do not compare ourselves with other people*. It is not about other people or how we measure up to them. It is about God and us. We stand alone before God.
- As we say these seven words, we *acknowledge that God is the source of our help*.

Whenever we pray the humility prayer—*God, be merciful to me, a sinner*—we give our lives to Christ. An evangelical friend once asked me in a very impassioned way, "Why don't you ask people to give their lives to Christ?" I was caught off guard in the moment, but here is my discernment about giving our lives to Christ. That phrase, "giving our lives to Christ," has been shaped in our time by television and popular media. "Giving our lives to Christ" in a television culture is something we have to do before the next commercial and the next sales pitch. And once we "give our lives to Christ," it is all over and done with. There is nothing more for us to do because the transaction has been completed.

According to the teachings of the New Testament, "giving our lives to Christ" is something that we need to do every single day, every single moment of our lives. Here's why. When we stop, when we think we have reached the pinnacle of our spiritual lives, we are in the greatest spiritual danger. When we think we have "arrived" in the spiritual life, we are tempted to think, "I'm better than other people. I don't need God." And in that moment we are lost; we are in danger; we are in trouble. If we are going to make our way in this life we will need to remember the seven words of the humility prayer: *God, be merciful to me, a sinner.*

If we are going to give our lives to and for Christ—every day, every moment—we are going to need continually to pray these words, *God, be merciful to me, a sinner.*

Spiritual Exercise

• In honest, straightforward language, compose your own "humility prayer."

SIN AS VIOLATION OF BOUNDARIES

If there is a prevailing stereotype about religion, it is that religion is a system of rules, regulations, and procedures. It has been said, "Everything begins in mysticism and ends in politics" (most often attributed to Charles Péguy). Laws and boundaries govern our lives. Gates, fences, and credentials restrain human activity. We all live by some system of rules, regulations, and procedures. Some are external: pay your taxes, recycle, educate your children, and maintain your property. Some are internal: eat balanced meals, keep away from danger, and smile politely at acquaintances in safe places. Some are both, such as: slow down when you come to a speed bump. If you don't, you are disobeying the *external* visual message, but you and your car may also suffer *internal* consequences.

A Culture of Conformity

All of us live with rules, regulations, and procedures. And we know that the way to get along in this world is to *conform*. We fit in. We keep most of the laws, more or less, right? We drive the speed limit, right? We stop at red lights, right? We conform, because if we don't there will be punishment, consequences.

Some of us grew up in a time when religion was mostly a matter of avoiding punishment and consequences. Religion was heavy on conformity. I served briefly, right out of school, in a mill village about forty-five minutes from my current home. One of the members of the church told me that he could recall a time when, if he missed Sunday school twice in a row, the foreman in his mill (who was not a member of his church) would call him into the office to ask if there was a problem!

Some of us grew up in a time when religion was mostly about *doing* the right things. When we did the right things there were good consequences—most of the time. And so, we conformed. We conformed to avoid the bad stuff, and we conformed to get more of the good stuff.

There is a powerful urge within us to conform. When we live in a culture of conformity something about our human nature wants to know the specific rules. What exactly am I supposed to do? What are the good things you want me to do? What are the bad things you want me to avoid?

The Ten Commandments

We bring these ingrained questions to our reading of the Ten Commandments (Exodus 20:1-17; also see Deuteronomy 5:6-21). The commandments, however, are about something different altogether. They are not our usual code of rules, regulations, and procedures. The commandments are a way that leads to life! They are not about getting the good stuff and avoiding the bad stuff. They are more complex than that. They are not about *conformity to laws*. They are about *formation of character*. They are not old words that should be pushed aside in our "enlightened" world. They are new and living words, as relevant as this morning's newspaper or last night's television news. We ignore them at our peril.

The commandments begin with a statement, not about what we are supposed to do, but about who is in charge, about who God is: "I am the LORD your God, who brought you out of the land of Egypt, out of the house of slavery" (Exodus 20:2). Imagine that you are a parent trying to get a point across to your children, and at some point you say, "I am your mother [I am your father]; I gave you life. Look at everything I have done for you."

God rescued Israel from slavery, freed it from oppression. "Remember me," God says, "Remember the burning bush and the Nile turned to blood and the cloud and fire and Pharaoh's army sinking in the sea and the manna every morning? Do you remember? Have you forgotten already?" Of course, we sometimes do forget. We need to be reminded. And we need to know the context of the commandments, because the One who is about to speak to us has a right to say whatever the Lord is going to say.

Spiritual Exercise

- As you prepare to make your confession to God, what is your image of God? What is God like? What is God's character? What is your history with God?

The First Tablet of the Law

The first four commandments are called the first tablet of the law, and they have to do with our relationship with God (Exodus 20:1-11).

I Am the LORD Your God . . . You Shall Have No Other Gods before Me.

There are ten commandments, and this is the first—*no other gods*—not the gods of Pharaoh's Egypt; not the gods of Canaanite pleasure; not the gods of Babylonian pleasure: *No Other Gods*.

This is the first commandment, and some of the rabbis argue that all of the other commandments are a commentary on this one. Whether you are speaking with first graders about to receive their Bibles, or with middle-school students in confirmation classes, or with high-school students on a retreat or in a small group setting, each of them is going to grow up and encounter other gods along the way. Someone—a professor, a friend, a coworker—will tell them, "You know, that's just one explanation; there are others. That's just one truth; there are others. That's just one God; there are others."

Do Not Make Idols

And there are other gods. There is a god of the marketplace. There is a god of sexuality. There is a god of warfare. There is a god of pleasure. There is a god of youth. We are commanded to have no other gods because there are other loyalties; other authorities—other gods—call to us. And we are tempted to build temples for these other gods, to make idols of them, and to bow down to them.

"When we reject the God of the Bible, we don't believe in nothing; we believe in everything" (attributed to G. K. Chesterton). "I see that you are very religious people," Paul said to those gathered in Athens (see Acts 17:16-34). And so, we hear the commandments clearly: You shall have no other gods; do not make idols; and then the third: do not take the Lord's name in vain—do not misuse the name of God.

Do Not Take the Lord's Name in Vain

How do we take the Lord's name in vain? In the Bible the name is the essence of the person. "Tell me your name," Jacob says to the One who wrestles with him (Genesis 32). "Tell me your name," Moses says to the One who meets him on holy ground (Exodus 3). God is very reluctant to give a name. Why? Because we are tempted to misuse that name, to assume that if we know God's name, we can use it in some way to our benefit. We assume that God is on our side, at our disposal, and in our pocket.

And so, we must say the name of God only with humility and reverence. The name of God is "above every name," Paul writes to the Philippians (2:9). The name is so holy that an observant Jew will neither speak it nor write it. We avoid taking the name of the Lord in vain by always asking, "Is what I am doing in the name and Spirit of God?" The answer: only God knows, and only God is the judge of that. We have killed in the name of God; pushed people out of the church in the name of God; done all sorts of things, holy and profane, in the name of God. No other gods . . . no idols . . . keep God's name holy.

Remember the Sabbath Day, and Keep It Holy

This is the next commandment. *Sabbath* means "to stop." There is nothing religious about the word *sabbath* (Hebrew, *shab-bat*). It simply means "to stop." Stop what you are doing. Why? Because, on the seventh day, God stopped and rested; literally God "caught his breath." The word *holy* means "different" or "set apart." Have one day in the week that is different from the other six. That is the command.

The Second Tablet of the Law

The second tablet contains the last six commandments (Exodus 20:12-17):

5. Honor your father and mother.
6. Do not murder or kill.
7. Do not commit adultery.
8. Do not bear false witness.
9. Do not steal.
10. Do not covet what belongs to your neighbor.

These six commandments order our lives with one another, and they are connected to the first four. God is the source, the foundation of our moral lives. We cannot separate religion and morality, believing and living. We cannot separate the first tablet—life with God—from the second tablet—life with one another. The last six commandments make life—everyday life, abundant life— possible. And here is the paradox: they make life possible *because they are restrictive*—only one husband or wife; only what belongs to you; only truth and not lies. They are restrictive because some things are in bounds and some things are out of bounds.

Boundaries Are Important

Why do we have boundaries? God must have felt that Israel needed boundaries in order to survive. Parents know instinctively about this. When our children are small we set clear boundaries: "Don't play in the street; don't even go near the street." Why? The street is no place for a child; it is dangerous; it is out of bounds. And so we make boundaries. Our children grow up. We set curfews. "Be in at a certain time." Why? Because nothing very constructive happens in the life of a teenager after a certain hour of the night. But that is just one father's perspective!

God says, "These are your boundaries." Do we go beyond them? Our human nature is to want to go beyond them. But we do not so much break the commandments as we break ourselves upon them. (See E. Stanley Jones, *Victorious Living* [New York: Abingdon Press, 1936], 20.) God makes these boundaries and says, "Live within them."

Why does the God who created the universe restrict us in this way? Why do we need these boundaries? Why can't we have it all? The boundaries have to do with our shortcomings and not with God's narrowness. I will sometimes go into a restaurant where there is a huge buffet. It's loaded with everything you can imagine. I sit down and someone brings a menu. My mind begins to move to a decision. There is something from my upbringing that says, "You need to get the most for your money. It's a buffet; it's all you can eat; go for it!"

But then another voice says, "It's too much, and you won't be able to restrain yourself." The culture we live in is a perpetual, 24/7, all-you-can-eat buffet. There is more work than we can do, more money than we can spend, more gods than we can worship, and more property than we can live on. We are tempted. We have always been tempted.

Our Jewish ancestors were given these laws, and of course, broke them. We all break them. And so the rabbis had an interesting response. They came up with 613 laws. A devout person would need to keep these 613 laws, and by so doing would not even get near the original ten laws. This has been called "building a fence around the law." Christians sometimes ridicule this practice, but we have our own way of building a fence around the law. I remember a phrase from my youth: "Don't drink or smoke or dance or chew or go out with girls who do."

Ultimately, building a fence around the law, making more laws, didn't help the Israelites. Then Jesus comes along and, as scholar Amy-Jill Levine suggests, does the very same thing in the Sermon on the Mount (Matthew 5–7):

> This is the Jesus who "makes a fence" . . . about the law to prevent transgression: rather than forbid murder, Jesus forbids hate (Matthew 5:21-22). Rather than forbid adultery, he forbids lust [vv. 27-28]. (*The Historical Jesus in Context* [Princeton, N.J.: Princeton University Press, 2006], 12.)

Jesus says that it is not about *conformity to law*, but about *formation of character*. It's not just "you shall not kill," but also don't be angry, for anger is the seed of murder. It's not just "you shall not commit adultery," but also do not think about someone who is not your husband or wife in a sexual way, for that is the seed of adultery.

Jesus knows that we sometimes do the right things—we conform—for the wrong reasons. And yet Jesus is clear. He comes not "to abolish the law . . . but to fulfill" (Matthew 5:17). We cannot live without the law, without boundaries. We are like children who need to learn, throughout our lives, about what is good and evil, about what is safe and what is dangerous.

When the Israelites received the commandments there was thunder and lightning, and they trembled. These laws are like thunder and lightning for us. We do not so much break them as we break ourselves upon them. You and I stand under the judgment of this law, these commandments. They did not go away when Jesus arrived on the scene.

As you frame prayers of confession, it will help to know the rich tradition of these ten commandments. The words shape and form us; they are God's way of leading us into life.

It is not that we need more information; the laws are pretty clear and the boundaries are quite visible. We do not need more *information*. We need *formation* in the character of Jesus, whose life was a fulfillment of the law. We are saved by grace through faith in his perfect obedience.

Spiritual Exercise

- Write a brief sentence of confession for each of the individual commandments:
  ○ You shall have no other gods.
  ○ You shall not make idols.
  ○ You shall not take the Lord's name in vain.
  ○ Remember the Sabbath and keep it holy.
  ○ Honor your father and mother.
  ○ Do not kill.
  ○ Do not commit adultery.
  ○ Do not steal.
  ○ Do not bear false witness.
  ○ Do not covet anything that belongs to your neighbor.

SIN AND THE POSSIBILITY OF FORGIVENESS

The relation of the confession of sin and the promise of assurance is not a simple one.

You have likely heard (or preached) sermons about forgiveness before. It might be good at the outset to let you in on what this meditation is *not* about. It's not going to tell you, "I understand forgiveness and I want to share what I know with you." It's not going to suggest, "I have *arrived* in the practice of forgiveness, like a guru coming down from the mountain." It's not a reflection that insists, "If we just worked harder at forgiveness we would be happier." And it is not teaching, "Some people just get it about forgiveness and some don't."

It might also be good to ask an honest question: So much is written, preached, and taught about forgiveness; where, exactly, has it gotten us? I want to attempt something more modest in this brief meditation. I want to say that forgiveness is a process that has three steps. And I want to say that all of us are somewhere on the journey of forgiveness. We are not yet there. We are on the way. I *am*, however, convinced that these three steps are the way to forgiveness.

Forgiveness as Need

Jesus teaches us to pray: Forgive us our debts [trespasses or sins], as we also have forgiven our debtors [those who trespass or sin against us]" (Matthew 6:12).

First, forgiveness is our *need*. This is the therapeutic meaning of forgiveness. We need to forgive others for our own sake. When we do not forgive others, we are the primary casualties. Martin Luther King Jr. once spoke of hate as a cancer that can destroy the one who hates. It is not all about what the other person deserves; we will get to that later. It is about *our need* to forgive.

Jesus is saying that there is something about forgiveness, our capacity to forgive, that is connected with his forgiveness of us. There is something about our grace toward others that is related to our living a grace-filled life.

But how do we forgive, practically? John Patton, a professor of pastoral counseling, has an insight that has been startling for me. He insists that forgiveness is not something we can achieve by trying harder. Forgiveness is not something we do. Forgiveness is something we discover.

If we focus on our own decision to forgive or not to forgive another person, it is likely that we will never do so. Patton says forgiveness is the discovery "that I am more like those who have hurt me than different from them. I am able to forgive when I discover that I am in *no position to forgive*" (*Is Human Forgiveness Possible?* [Nashville: Abingdon Press, 1985], 16; emphasis added).

Our inability to forgive holds us captive. If you want to see this in Scripture, read the parable of the unforgiving servant (Matthew 18:23-35). The Latin word for *mercy* is *eleison*, related to our English word *liaison* or *bond*. Christians around the world chant the prayer *Kyrie Eleison*, "Lord have mercy." When we refuse to forgive we hold others and ourselves in bondage. When we forgive we loosen the attachments, freeing the other person and ourselves in the process.

Jesus spoke the Aramaic language, and when we meditate on the Aramaic version of the Lord's Prayer (see Matthew 6:9-13; Luke 11:2-4), we can hear this familiar prayer in a new way:

Loose the cords of mistakes binding us
> as we release the strands we hold of others' guilt.

Lighten our load of secret debts
> as we relieve others of their need to repay.

Forgive our hidden past, the secret shames,
> as we consistently forgive what others hide.

When we forgive we release the other person, and in the process *we* are released. As we understand our own forgiveness, we discover forgiveness for others. The bonds are loosened. The hate is tossed to the winds. We forgive because God forgives our sins. We are not God. We are forgiven sinners—all of us. Forgiveness is our *need*.

Forgiveness as Witness

Second, forgiveness is our *witness*. Forgiveness is an essential dimension of the Christian faith that makes our witness as a community possible. Without forgiveness there is no family, no community, and no church. None of us is perfect. At First United Methodist Church in Oklahoma City the congregation gathered for worship on the Sunday after the horrible bombing of April 19, 1995. In addition to the enormous human travesty, their beautiful sanctuary, on the historic registry, was in a shambles; they faced massive renovation. In the midst of death and grief, fear and loss, the people were in shock. Nick Harris, the pastor, made this statement in a sermon: "We have to pray for the people who did this. If we don't, we're not a church; we're a social club."

The Christian church, gathered for worship, is not a social club. We are a community of forgiven and forgiving sinners, saved by the grace of God. This is the *evangelical* value of forgiveness. Now, the common stereotype of an evangelical in our culture is someone who is judgmental; maybe someone who has conservative political convictions; maybe even someone who is mean spirited. But authentic evangelical witness is all about the good news of forgiveness and how we are compelled to share that good news with others. At the end of Luke's Gospel, Jesus says,

> "Thus it is written, that the Messiah is to suffer and to rise from the dead on the third day, and that repentance and *forgiveness of sins* is to be proclaimed in his name to all nations, beginning from Jerusalem" (24:46-47, emphasis added).

Do you think forgiveness can be a witness? In the aftermath of the Civil War, Abraham Lincoln was urged to punish the South. His response, "Do I not destroy my enemies when I make them my friends?" provides a powerful witness to forgiveness (Philip Yancey, *What's So Amazing about Grace?* [Grand Rapids: Zondervan, 1997], 130).

We forgive because we have a need to forgive. This is truth, and it is truth you might hear from Oprah or Dr. Phil. It is one step in the journey, but it is not the fullness of forgiveness.

We forgive because this is our witness. Here it gets more difficult. Here followers of Jesus depart from the practices of insurgents and diplomats; here followers of Jesus read the Sermon on the Mount and realize that we forgive *before* the other party is worthy of our forgiveness. Jesus taught the Lord's Prayer to people who lived in the precise location on our planet where retaliation had replaced forgiveness, and where, even today, innocents suffer from the decisions of those who live great distances away—in Baghdad and Tehran and Washington and Jerusalem.

Why did Jesus teach the people to pray these words? It turns out these would be words he would not only *speak* but also *live*. And that leads to another basic truth.

16

Forgiveness as Good News

Forgiveness is our *need*.

Forgiveness is our *witness*.

Forgiveness is our *gospel*.

In Jesus Christ, God has forgiven our sins. Paul writes to the Romans, in 5:8: "God proves his love for us in that *while we still were sinners* Christ died for us" (emphasis added).

None of us is so far along that we do not need to be reminded of this basic truth. We are forgiven, reconciled sinners, saved by the grace of God. I love this verse in Charles Wesley's hymn "O for a Thousand Tongues to Sing": "He breaks the power of cancelled sin, he sets the prisoner free!"

That is what it means to be a Christian: to know that I have been released from my own sin, my own guilt, and my own failures, through the life, death, and resurrection of Jesus Christ. And that is our starting place; we all stand in need of God's forgiveness. As a Sunday school teacher once said to me, "The ground is level at the foot of the cross." That is the mind-altering, consciousness-shaping, ego-reducing reality of what it means to be a Christian: to know that I am not perfect, just forgiven.

The years come and go in families, and we sometimes find ourselves in the emergency room—kidney stones, allergic reactions, injuries playing softball and basketball and running through the house—add your own experiences to the list. When I'm there I look around the waiting area. Some of the folk are young; some are old. Some are rich; some are poor. Some speak English; some speak Spanish. Some are black; some are white. You can look at some of the people and immediately you know what is wrong. Looking at others, you aren't so sure. But you know, beneath the surface, that they all have some need or they wouldn't be there.

Spiritual Exercise

- Write a prayer of confession that explores the human condition of those whom you observe and live with this day.

A good friend recently reminded me that the church is not a school for saints but a *hospital for sinners*. Could it be that many of us today have made our way to this hospital for sinners because we have something wrong with us that will not go away and it has to do with forgiveness?

Maybe we need to forgive someone else. Maybe we need to ask someone else's forgiveness. Maybe we need to forgive ourselves. Maybe we need to hear that God has forgiven us.

There is urgency about forgiveness. In the revivalist tradition of my childhood, it might be expressed in this way:

- Don't leave this place (or moment) unless you have wrestled with this prayer of Jesus: "Forgive us our sins, as we forgive those who sin against us."
- Don't leave this place (or moment) unless you know deep within that you are forgiven, through the grace of God that is greater than all your sin.
- Don't leave this place (or moment) unless you have begun to loose the cords that connect you with someone who needs your forgiveness.

The church *is* a hospital for sinners. We forgive because we *need* to forgive. We forgive because that is our *witness*. Indeed, the world has never been more in need of Christians who bear witness to forgiveness. And we forgive because that is the heart of the *gospel*. "God proves his love for us in that while we still were sinners Christ died for us."

Brothers and sisters, in the name of Jesus Christ, and through the power of his cross, we are *forgiven!*

CHAPTER TWO

CONFESSION, ASSURANCE, AND THE HUMAN CONDITION

DEPENDENCE ON GOD

Choral or Congregational Call to Prayer
"I Need Thee Every Hour," by Annie S. Hawks (verse 1)

Invitation
Let us come before the Lord in spirit and in truth.
✞ *Silence*

Prayer of Confession
Holy and gracious God,
  we confess that we have sinned against you
  and missed your purpose for our lives.
Some of our sin is known to us—
  the thoughts and words and deeds
    of which we are ashamed.
Some of our sin is known only to you.

19

In the name of Jesus Christ,
    we ask for deliverance, forgiveness, and restoration.
✞ *Silence*

Words of Assurance

If we say we have no sin,
    we deceive ourselves.
But if we confess our sin,
    God is faithful and just to forgive our sin
    and cleanse us from all unrighteousness.
Thanks be to God! Amen.

SEEKING GUIDANCE

Choral or Congregational Call to Prayer
"I Have Decided to Follow Jesus," by Anonymous

Invitation
Let us with faith and confidence
    kneel before the One who leads, guides,
        and sustains us.
✝ *Silence*

Prayer of Confession
O God,
    in these perplexing days we ask
    that you would increase our faith;
    that you would enlarge our capacity to forgive;
    that you would guide our stumbling feet
        in the way that leads to life.
Forgive us when we are tempted to give up,
    and sustain us in the journey toward the cross.
Through Jesus Christ our Lord . . .
✝ *Silence*

Words of Assurance
The One who began a good work in you
    will be faithful to complete it.
In the name of Jesus Christ
    you are being redeemed. Amen.

IN RESPONSE TO WORLD HUNGER

For scriptural context, read John 6.

Choral or Congregational Call to Prayer

"Take Our Bread," by Joe Wise (refrain, sing twice)

Invitation

Jesus said, "I am the bread of life.
Whoever comes to me will never be hungry,
  and whoever believes in me will never be thirsty."
Let us confess our dependence upon the One
  who nourishes and sustains us.
✢ *Silence*

Prayer of Confession

O God, you invite us to feast at your table,
  and we reject your invitation.
You call us to taste your goodness,
  and we turn away to other gods.
You command us to share your bounty with others,
  and we consume at the expense of our neighbors.
For those of us who are hungry,
  O God, give bread.
And for those of us who have bread,
  give us a hunger for justice and righteousness;
    through Jesus Christ, the bread of life, we pray. Amen.
✢ *Silence*

Words of Assurance

Jesus promised,
"Blessed are those who hunger and thirst
  for justice and righteousness,
    for they will be filled."
Whoever eats of this bread will live forever.
In his name we are sustained,
  in this life and in the life to come. Amen.

IN RESPONSE TO APATHY

Choral or Congregational Call to Prayer

"Spirit of the Living God," by Daniel Iverson (sing twice)

Invitation

Let us come into the presence of the One
    who is joy and peace.
☩ *Silence*

Prayer of Confession

O God,
we have lived without regard to the limitations
    you have placed upon us.
Forgive us.
We have acted as if we are alone
    in our service to others.
Have mercy upon us.
We have neglected the means of grace,
    which nourish and sustain us.
Forgive us, and have mercy upon us.
Draw near to your people,
    restore our souls,
    and grant us your peace.
☩ *Silence*

Words of Assurance

Believe the good news:
    the dwelling of God is with men and women.
The One who redeems Israel will be our God,
    and we will be God's people.
The steadfast love of the Lord is from everlasting
    to everlasting.
Thanks be to God! Amen.

IN THE MIDST OF DESPAIR

For scriptural context, read Philippians 4.

Choral or Congregational Call to Prayer

"Jesus, the Very Thought of Thee," attr. to Bernard of Clairvaux,
12th cent.; trans. by Edward Caswall (st. 2)

Invitation

Let us come before the Lord,
    who promises to make all things new.
♱ *Silence*

Prayer of Confession

O God, you have begun a good work in us,
    and you are faithful to complete it.
And yet our pessimism about what *is*
    often overwhelms our optimism about what is to come.
Open our hearts,
    that we might trust in your gracious providence.
Open our minds,
    that we might believe in your mighty power.
Open our eyes,
    that we might see the coming kingdom,
        for which we pray.
Forgive us for failures of imagination, vision, and hope.
Increase our faith.
♱ *Silence*

Words of Assurance

Brothers and sisters,
    believe the good news.
Have no anxiety about anything,
    but in everything by prayer and supplication
    with thanksgiving
        let your requests be made known to God.
And the peace of God,
    which surpasses all understanding,
    will keep your hearts and minds in Christ Jesus. Amen.

SELF-SUFFICIENCY AND PRIDE

For scriptural context, read Psalm 23.

Choral or Congregational Call to Prayer

"The King of Love, My Shepherd Is," by Henry W. Baker (verse 1)

Invitation

Let us acknowledge the One who provides for us.
✦ *Silence*

Prayer of Confession

God of creation, giver of life:
    we confess our anxiety about this very day,
        which you have made.
Forgive us.
Lord Jesus Christ, bread of life:
    we acknowledge our refusal to receive the grace
        that sustains us.
Have mercy upon us.
Holy Spirit, giver of new life,
    we declare the limitations of our energies;
        our resources; our gifts.
Grant us your peace.
✦ *Silence*

Words of Assurance

Hear the good news:
God leads us beside still waters and restores our souls,
    and in God's presence there is sanctuary.
Let us give thanks for the eternal presence of the One
    who is life and peace.
Amen.

DISOBEDIENCE

For scriptural context, read, Psalm 46.

Choral or Congregational Call to Prayer
"Through It All," by Andraé Crouch (sing twice)

Invitation
Let us bow before Almighty God,
   our strength and our redeemer.
✝ *Silence*

Prayer of Confession
Almighty and gracious God,
   we have wandered from your ways,
   following the desires of our own hearts.
Forgive us.
We have broken your laws,
   through the evil that we have done
   and the good that we have left undone.
Have mercy upon us.
We have trusted in our own righteousness
   and neglected the way of the cross,
   which leads to life.
Grant us your peace,
   through Jesus Christ.
✝ *Silence*

Words of Assurance
Believe the good news:
   the Lord is our refuge and strength,
   a very present help in trouble.
Deliver us from ourselves,
O Lord,
   and lead us in paths of righteousness,
   for thy name's sake. Amen.

JUDGMENTALISM

For scriptural context, read Romans 5.

Choral or Congregational Call to Prayer

"Grace Greater than Our Sin," by Julia H. Johnston (st. 1)

Invitation

Let us drink from the well of mercy;
    let us touch the garment of the One who would heal us;
    let us not be blinded by our own sin,
        so that we might see others with compassion.
✟ *Silence*

Prayer of Confession

O God, we confess an unwillingness to see the world
        that you have created.
We look upon others in judgment
    and upon ourselves with either arrogance
        or self-condemnation.
We critique the faults of others,
    even as we avoid the flaws that are within us.
Be thou our vision, O Lord.
Help us see you more clearly,
    love you more dearly,
    and follow you more nearly,
        day by day.
✟ *Silence*

Words of Assurance

Believe the good news:
God shows his love for us in that
    while we were yet sinners
Christ died for us.
In the name of Jesus Christ,
    and through the power of his cross,
    we are forgiven. Amen.

EXHAUSTION

For scriptural context, read Ephesians 2.

Choral or Congregational Call to Prayer

"Spirit of the Living God," by Daniel Iverson (sing twice)

Invitation

Let us enter in the presence of the One
 whose yoke is easy, whose burden is light.
☩ *Silence*

Prayer of Confession

O God,
We live as if we are not your beloved children.
We silence the voices that call us your good creation.
We seek salvation in good deeds.
We cannot imagine that you love us for who we are,
 instead of what we can do.
For our unbelief in your love,
 forgive us.
For our neglect of your grace,
 have mercy upon us.
For our narrowness of spirit and hardness of heart,
 grant us your peace.
☩ *Silence*

Words of Assurance

Believe the good news:
"Not my power, nor my might,
 but by my Spirit," says the Lord.
Trust in God's goodness,
 and rely upon God's strength. Amen.

AFTER A NATURAL DISASTER

For scriptural context, read Psalm 46.

Choral or Congregational Call to Prayer

"Stand by Me," by Charles Albert Tindley (st. 1)

Invitation

Let us be in silence before the One
who creates and redeems us.

✛ *Silence*

Prayer of Confession

O God, the storms of life are raging.
The signs of death and devastation are all around us.
We are overwhelmed by human need,
and quick to cast blame or judgment.
We ask for your calm; your presence;
your peace; your strength.
Help us pass through the storms,
and guide all of your people safely
into the promised land.
O God, the storms of life are raging,
and yet, we believe that you are our help in ages past
and our hope for years to come.

✛ *Silence*

Words of Assurance

Believe the good news:
God is our refuge and strength,
a very present help in times of trouble.
Be of good courage;
strengthen the weak;
trust in the goodness of God,
who loves the poor and hears their cries. Amen.

CONFUSION

For scriptural context, read Proverbs 3.

Choral or Congregational Call to Prayer

"He Leadeth Me, O Blessed Thought," by Joseph H. Gilmore (st. 1)

Invitation

Let us listen for the voice of the One
  who leads us in paths of righteousness,
  for his name's sake.
☦ *Silence*

Prayer of Confession

O God,
  to repent is to turn away from everything
    that separates us from you.
We are imperfect people,
  and yet you love us.
We are distracted people,
  and yet you come near to us.
We are lost,
  and yet you find us.
Draw near to us,
  in your saving presence and power,
  through Jesus Christ our Lord.
☦ *Silence*

Words of Assurance

Hear the good news:
God is the alpha and the omega;
  the beginning and the end;
  the first and the last.
The One who calls you is the One
  who walks beside you
  to give you strength and peace.
Amen.

ACKNOWLEDGING BROKENNESS

Choral or Congregational Call to Prayer

"There Is a Fountain," by William Cowper (st. 1)

Invitation

With all of our strength and with all of our might,
   let us pray unto the Lord.
✢ *Silence*

Prayer of Confession

Lord, listen to your children praying.
We confess our failures
   and call upon your strength.
We acknowledge our brokenness
   and cry out for your healing.
We examine ourselves
   and our sin is clearly before us.
Hear our prayers that are too deep for words.
Lord, listen to your children praying.
✢ *Silence*

Words of Assurance

Thus says the Lord,
"I have heard the cries of my people,
   and I have come down to deliver them."
Believe the good news:
   in the name of Jesus Christ,
   we are set free from the power of sin and given new life.
Glory to God! Amen.

REBELLION

Choral or Congregational Call to Prayer

"Open My Eyes That I May See," by Clara H. Scott (st. 1)

Invitation

The Lord delights in a humble spirit.
Let us listen for a word that is beyond us.
Let us receive a power that is above us.
Let us resonate with a peace that is within us.
✝ *Silence*

Prayer of Confession

O God,
You create us in your image,
   and yet we rebel against your love.
You take our sins upon yourself, in Jesus,
   and yet we reject your grace.
You pour your Spirit upon us,
   and yet we resist your gifts.
Teach us the way of humility.
Through the power of the cross,
   have mercy upon us
   and forgive us.
✝ *Silence*

Words of Assurance

Hear the good news:
In the name of Jesus Christ,
   who lived among us as a servant,
   and who died on the cross for our sake,
     we are forgiven.
Glory to God!
Amen.

AFTER A SENSELESS TRAGEDY

Choral or Congregational Call to Prayer

"When Our Confidence Is Shaken," by Fred Pratt Green (st. 1)

Invitation

Let us confess our dependence on the One
    who is our refuge and our strength.
✟ *Silence*

Prayer of Confession

O God, in a time filled with violence and devastation,
    we confess anxiety about the world in which we live.
We lack the resources to see the present with clarity
    or the future with hope.
We have grown numb to the loss of life,
    and we are too eager to retaliate.
Forgive us.
We have been quick to cast blame on others
    and less inclined to consider the anger
    that is within our own hearts.
Have mercy on us.
Grant us solidarity with all who suffer,
    compassion for all who grieve,
    and patience toward all who serve the common good.
Cleanse the thoughts of our hearts and minds
    with the peace that surpasses human understanding,
    through Jesus Christ our Savior.
✟ *Silence*

Words of Assurance

Hear the good news:
    even in the valley of the shadow of death, God is with us.
Let us claim the promise
    that nothing in life or in death will be able to separate us
        from the love of God,
    through Christ Jesus our Lord. Amen.

FOR RENEWAL OF LIFE

Choral or Congregational Call to Prayer

"Lord, I Want to Be a Christian," African American Spiritual (st. 1)

Invitation

Let us draw near, by faith,
    to the One who has first come to us,
    in Jesus Christ,
    the word made flesh,
    full of grace and truth.
✝ *Silence*

Prayer of Confession

O God, you create us for relationship.
And yet we are isolated from one another
    and separated from you.
We confess that our self-sufficiency leads to loneliness,
    and our self-improvement leads to exhaustion.
Anoint us with the power of your Holy Spirit;
    connect us to the One body, the church,
    and to the Lord of the church,
Jesus Christ, who comes to set the captives free.
✝ *Silence*

Words of Assurance

Hear the good news:
    by grace you have been saved through faith,
        and this is the gift of God,
    not the result of works,
        lest anyone should boast.
In the name of Jesus Christ,
    and through his gracious life, death, and resurrection,
        we are forgiven. Amen.

FOR A RENEWED SENSE OF PURPOSE

Choral or Congregational Call to Prayer
"Marching to Zion," by Isaac Watts; refrain by Robert Lowry (st. 1)

Invitation
Let the power of the spirit shape the prayers of God's people.
Let us pray.
✝ *Silence*

Prayer of Confession
Lord Jesus, you call us to follow.
We are at times hesitant,
    unsure of our direction;
    uncertain of our commitment;
    unwilling to count the cost.
And yet you continue to call us,
    out of darkness and into light;
    out of bondage and into freedom;
    out of death and into life.
Where we have resisted your call and claim upon us,
    we ask for forgiveness;
where we have taken a small step toward you,
    encourage us;
and where we have seen a glimpse of the future
    that you have prepared for us,
    draw near.
✝ *Silence*

Words of Assurance
The Lord is our shepherd,
    and therefore we lack nothing.
The Lord leads us beside still waters and restores our souls.
The Lord leads us in paths of righteousness,
    for his name's sake.
Let us walk with the Lord,
    who promises to be with us, always. Amen.

SEEKING CLARITY

Choral or Congregational Call to Prayer

"Trust and Obey," by John H. Sammis (st. 2)

Invitation

Let us slow down;
let us be in step with the One
    who walks with us in the journey.
✠ *Silence*

Prayer of Confession

Gracious Lord, you walk with us in this life,
    and yet at times we are distracted
    and do not know that you are with us.
We confess our inability to see you;
    our unwillingness to hear you;
    our hesitation in following you.
And yet we believe that you are indeed present among us,
    mysteriously,
        in this very time and place.
Open our eyes, our ears, our hearts, and our hands.
Help us stop, rest, listen, and learn.
Make us receptive to your presence,
    through Jesus Christ our risen Lord.
✠ *Silence*

Words of Assurance

Lord Jesus,
    you are God with us—
Emmanuel.
You call us not only disciples,
    but also friends.
Draw near to us, abide with us,
    and renew us in your image. Amen.

SEEKING GOD'S WILL

Choral or Congregational Call to Prayer

"Jesus Calls Us," by Cecil Frances Alexander (st. 1)

Invitation

O Lord,
> give us ears to hear what you are saying to us.

✟ *Silence*

Prayer of Confession

O God,
> we seek you, and yet we hide from you.

At times we draw near,
> and at other times we move away.

If we are honest,
> we sometimes prefer darkness to light;
>> despair to hope;
>> confusion to clarity.

Help us receive the call to rebirth as a gift,
> and open our hearts and minds
> to the Spirit that makes all things new.

Through Jesus Christ our Lord.

✟ *Silence*

Words of Assurance

Brothers and sisters,
> hear the good news.

The kingdom of God has come near.
Repent, and believe the gospel.
In the name of Jesus,
> you are forgiven.

Amen.

DEPLETION

Choral or Congregational Call to Prayer

"Fill My Cup, Lord," by Richard Blanchard (sing twice)

Invitation

Let us draw near to the One who is gracious and merciful,
slow to anger, and abounding in steadfast love.
✞ *Silence*

Prayer of Confession

O God,
you are the hope of all who seek you
and the help of all who find you.
We thirst for a grace that can be found only in Jesus Christ.
If our wells are dry,
if our spirits are weary,
if our hearts are hardened,
forgive us, we pray,
and restore to us the joy of your salvation.
✞ *Silence*

Words of Assurance

Blessed are those who hunger and thirst for righteousness,
for they shall be satisfied.
It is the desire to please you that pleases you, O God.
Fill us with your peace,
and make us whole. Amen.

FOR INCREASED COMPASSION

Choral or Congregational Call to Prayer

"Love Divine, All Loves Excelling," by Charles Wesley (st. 2)

Invitation

Let us listen for the sound of God's voice.
In quietness and stillness,
    let us tune our hearts to the rhythm of God's grace.
✢ *Silence*

Prayer of Confession

O God,
    we confess a hardness of heart
    and a narrowness of vision.
The wideness of your mercy surrounds us,
    but we are not receptive to your presence.
Your love is broader than the measure of our minds,
    but we do not have eyes to see your kingdom.
Maker of heaven and earth,
    finish your new creation
    and overcome our creaturely rebellion.
Lord Jesus,
    who art all compassion,
    draw near to us
    and to the world for whom you have died.
Giver of life,
    pour out your Spirit on all flesh.
✢ *Silence*

Words of Assurance

Brothers and sisters, believe the good news:
God is love.
As children of God,
    let us live in God's love,
    and let us share God's love with one another.
Amen.

DISCOURAGEMENT

Choral or Congregational Call to Prayer

"O for a Thousand Tongues to Sing," by Charles Wesley (st. 4)

Invitation

Let us come into God's presence with honesty
    about who we are,
    but also with hopefulness about who we might become
        through the work of grace.
☦ *Silence*

Prayer of Confession

O God,
    we confess our faith and trust in you,
    but also our inability to see your purpose;
        our failure to receive your gifts;
        our resistance to your grace.
Remove the obstacles that separate us from you.
Remind us of your steadfast love for us.
Rekindle the fire of your spirit that dwells deep within us.
We ask in the name of Jesus Christ.
☦ *Silence*

Words of Assurance

The Lord is our strength and our deliverer.
If the Lord has set you free,
    you are free indeed.
In the name of Jesus Christ,
    and through the power of his cross,
    you are forgiven.
Glory to God.
Amen.

WEARINESS OF SOUL

Choral or Congregational Call to Prayer

"Have Thine Own Way, Lord," by Adelaide A. Pollard (st. 2)

Invitation

God opposes the proud.
God gives grace to the humble.
Let us bow before the Lord our maker.
✠ *Silence*

Prayer of Confession

O God, we approach you with hesitation and ambivalence:
  we confess to hardness of heart,
    poverty of spirit, and weariness of soul.
We have resisted your grace,
    depending instead on our own virtues.
We have rejected your laws,
    following instead the desires of our own hearts.
We live at some distance from the life-giving mercy
    that would renew us.
Hear our prayers, spoken and unspoken.
Draw near to us
    and grant us the peace of communion
      with you and all your people.
Through Jesus Christ our Lord . . .
✠ *Silence*

Words of Assurance

"Come unto me," Jesus says,
"All of you who labor and are carrying heavy burdens,
    and I will give you rest.
"For my yoke is easy,
    and my burden is light."
Let us hear the good news of God's gracious invitation.
Let us receive the gift of abundant life. Amen.

UNFAITHFULNESS

Choral or Congregational Call to Prayer

"He Is Lord," from Philippians 2:9-11

Invitation

Let us consider the faithfulness of the God
who keeps covenant with us,
who creates, redeems, and sustains us.
✣ *Silence*

Prayer of Confession

Liberating God,
we have tasted your freedom,
and we have preferred bondage.
Forgive us.
We have journeyed to sanctuary,
and we have wandered from your ways.
Have mercy on us.
We have prospered in abundance,
and we have taken your blessings for granted.
O God, our help in ages past,
our hope for years to come,
grant us your peace,
through Jesus Christ our Lord. Amen.
✣ *Silence*

Words of Assurance

The promises of God are true and worthy
of our trust and confidence.
God is faithful
to forgive us and to cleanse us from all unrighteousness.
Amen.

ESTRANGEMENT

Choral or Congregational Call to Prayer

"Guide Me, O Thou Great Jehovah," by William Williams (st. 1)

Invitation

Come let us walk in the light of the Lord.
✟ *Silence*

Prayer of Confession

O God,
   you place within our hearts a desire to see the future
      and to move toward it.
And yet we sometimes find ourselves slow to respond
      to your invitations;
      hesitant to hear your callings;
      fearful of required changes;
      stuck in addictive patterns of living.
The distance between who we are
      and who you call us to be is wearying.
Give us renewed eagerness to live in hope
      and to follow in your steps,
         through Jesus Christ our Lord. Amen.
✟ *Silence*

Words of Assurance

The One who calls us is also the One who sustains us.
Hear the good news:
"Come unto me," Jesus said,
   "all of you who labor and are heavy laden,
      and I will give you rest."
Amen.

LACK OF DEDICATION

Choral or Congregational Call to Prayer

"A Charge to Keep I Have," by Charles Wesley (st. 4)

Invitation

Let us be quiet,
 let us be silent,
 and let us listen for the still, small voice.
♰ *Silence*

Prayer of Confession

O Lord,
 forgive us for the sins of this and every season:
  we place second matters first;
  we sit at a feast and yet hunger for your spirit;
  we become aware that the vessels of our hearts
  cannot contain the fullness of your grace.
Remove from us all that competes with your way for us.
Quiet us down,
 that we may be still and know that you are God.
In silence may we hear your Word with new clarity,
 and may we keep it with new intensity,
 for the sake of Jesus Christ, our Savior.
♰ *Silence*

Words of Assurance

Believe the good news:
Salvation comes not through human striving,
 but as divine gift.
In Jesus Christ, the way, the truth, and the life,
 we are made whole.
Amen.

CHAPTER THREE

CONFESSION, ASSURANCE, AND THE HOLY SCRIPTURES

GENESIS 1–2

Choral or Congregational Call to Prayer

"For the Fruits of This Creation," by Fred Pratt Green (st. 3)

Invitation

Let us confess our sin before the God who is
  holy and merciful; strong and vulnerable;
  judging and gracious.
☦ Silence

Prayer of Confession

O God, you created us in your image
  and breathed into us the breath of life.
You have given order to the chaos of this world,
  separating light and dark; sabbath and work;
  planting and harvest; life and death.
And yet at times we violate your boundaries:
  our labor exceeds the measure of our energies;

our worship is limited to the attention of our minds;
our rest is inadequate for the demands placed upon us;
our souls grow weary in our work on behalf of others.
O Thou, who guides the seasons of life, slow us down.
Let the works of our hands be pleasing in your sight.
Let the prayers of our hearts rise like incense to you.
Through Jesus Christ our Lord, we pray.
✟ *Silence*

Words of Assurance

For everything there is a time and a season
    and a purpose under heaven,
and God has made all things beautiful in their own time.
The one who created you will sustain you
through the presence and power of the Holy Spirit. Amen.

Genesis 3

Choral or Congregational Call to Prayer

"Blessed Be the God of Israel," by Michael Perry (st. 1)

Invitation

Let us call upon the mercies of the God
who creates and redeems us.

♱ *Silence*

Prayer of Confession

God of creation and God of the Exodus,
at times we are overwhelmed by the evil
that exists in this world.
At times we are indifferent to the ruthless oppression
that scars the lives of countless people.
At times we are tempted to lose hope
that goodness and righteousness will prevail.
Forgive our apathy;
our inattention;
our unbelief.
Remind us of your strong desire to deliver us from evil.
Through Jesus Christ, we pray.

♱ *Silence*

Words of Assurance

The Lord spoke and called all creation into being.
The Lord spoke and called all things good.
Only say the word, O Lord,
and we shall be healed.
Amen.

EXODUS 3

Choral or Congregational Call to Prayer

"Surely the Presence of the Lord," by Lanny Wolfe (sing twice)

Invitation

Let us take off our shoes,
　for we are standing on holy ground.
✟ *Silence*

Prayer of Confession

Gracious God,
　you are always present,
　　always near,
and yet at times we do not see you in the burning bush;
　we do not know that we stand on holy ground.
Gracious God,
　you often speak to us,
　　at times calling us by name,
and yet we do not discern your voice
　in the midst of everyday noise and chatter.
Forgive our distracted minds and hardened hearts.
Through Jesus Christ, our Lord, we beseech you.
✟ *Silence*

Words of Assurance

"If you seek me with all your heart," says the Lord,
　"you will find me."
The glory of God is revealed to us
　in the face of Jesus Christ, our Lord and Savior.
Amen.

EXODUS 13

Choral or Congregational Call to Prayer

"Trust and Obey," by John H. Sammis (st. 1)

Invitation

Let us trust in the God whose providence is trustworthy,
   whose love is steadfast, and whose grace is everlasting.
✟ *Silence*

Prayer of Confession

O God,
   you promise to be with us always.
And yet we forget that you are present,
   walking beside us;
   guiding our steps;
   leading us forward.
If we think that we are on our own,
   draw near.
If we know that we are lost,
   help us see the signs:
   a cloud by day, a fire by night.
Forgive us, for we are easily led astray.
Show us the paths of righteousness,
   and we will walk in them.
Through Jesus Christ,
   the way, the truth, and the life, we pray.
✟ *Silence*

Words of Assurance

The One who creates and sustains the universe
   knows us by name and acts on our behalf
      with providence and purpose.
Believe the good news, brothers and sisters:
God is with us!
Thanks be to God.

1 KINGS 19

Choral or Congregational Call to Prayer

"Where He Leads Me, I Will Follow," by E. W. Blandy (st. 1)

Invitation

God is Spirit.
Let us come into the presence of the God who is
    Spirit and Truth.
✟ *Silence*

Prayer of Confession

O God,
    we gather as a people sometimes confused
    and sometimes overwhelmed.
There are so many options before us:
    some lead to life, others to death.
The seductive and persuasive messages of our culture
    sometimes drown out the still, small voice
    that calms our fears and purifies our motivations.
Where we have neglected your word,
    forgive us.
Where we have resisted the promptings of your Spirit,
    have mercy upon us, and grant us the peace
    that the world can neither give nor take away.
✟ *Silence*

Words of Assurance

Leader: Jesus says, "Peace, I leave with you,
    my peace I give to you."
Brothers and sisters, the good news is near to you.
The grace is within you; the voice is calling you.
Believe the good news:
You are loved, forgiven, and reconciled.
People: In the name of Christ,
    you are loved, forgiven, and reconciled.
All: Thanks be to God!

PSALM 23

Choral or Congregational Call to Prayer

"The King of Love, My Shepherd Is," by Henry W. Baker (st. 1)

Invitation

Let us pay attention to the One who is
   always watching over us.
☫ *Silence*

Prayer of Confession

O God,
   you provide everything that we need,
   and yet we lack the one thing necessary.
You restore our souls,
   and yet we are overwhelmed by choices
   and exhausted by demands.
You lead us in the right direction,
   and yet we wander after trivial pursuits.
You are with us in the dark places,
   and yet we sense that we are alone.
Speak to us, Good Shepherd.
Guide us, protect us,
   and lead us to the sources of life and peace.
☫ *Silence*

Words of Assurance

Believe the good news:
The Good Shepherd is always nearer to us
   than we are to ourselves.
In the name of Jesus Christ,
   we are embraced, loved, and forgiven.
Glory to God! Amen.

PSALM 46

Choral or Congregational Call to Prayer

"O God; Our Help in Ages Past," by Isaac Watts (st. 2)

Invitation

Let us seek shelter in the One who is our help
and our salvation,
even Jesus Christ our Savior.
✟ *Silence*

Prayer of Confession

O God,
you are the help of all who seek you
and the hope of all who find you.
And yet at times our eyes are blind to your presence
and our trust is placed in principalities and powers
that lead us astray.
Draw near to us.
Correct us.
Inspire us.
Enlighten us.
Move us to acknowledge your holiness,
and let us stand amazed in your presence.
This we ask in the name of Jesus Christ.
Amen.
✟ *Silence*

Words of Assurance

Surely it is God who saves us.
Let us trust in the Lord and not be afraid.
Thanks be to God!

PSALM 51

Choral or Congregational Call to Prayer

"Be Thou My Vision," ancient Irish; trans. by Mary E. Byrne; versed by Eleanor H. Hull, alt. (st. 1, substitute "our" for "my")

Invitation

Let us pray to the Lord with humility.
Let us consider the greatness of God
    alongside our need for a new heart and a new spirit.
✤ *Silence*

Prayer of Confession

O God of glory and mercy,
    you reveal yourself to us in Jesus.
And yet at times our eyes do not see him;
    our minds do not know him;
    our hearts to do not love him;
    our voices do not praise him.
Be thou our vision, O Lord:
    expand our perception,
    increase our comprehension,
    strengthen our passion,
    and transform us through acts of worship and service.
In the name of the One whose light shines in the darkness,
    even Jesus Christ our Lord, we pray.
✤ *Silence*

Words of Assurance

You cleanse our hearts, O God.
You make us new creatures.
You fill us with your Holy Spirit.
We give you thanks and praise,
    through Jesus Christ our Lord. Amen.

PSALM 119

Choral or Congregational Call to Prayer

"Thy Word," by Amy Grant (sing twice)

Invitation

Let us incline our ears to wisdom
and our hearts to the Lord.
☦ *Silence*

Prayer of Confession

O God,
When we wander far
    from your purpose for our lives—
Be thou our vision.
When we neglect your means of grace—
May our souls thirst for you.
When we resist your teaching—
Let your word be a lamp to our feet and a light to our path.
In the confusion,
    amid the fighting without and the fears within,
    help us listen for your voice,
    that we might walk in your ways
        to the glory of your name.
☦ *Silence*

Words of Assurance

The One who keeps Israel neither slumbers nor sleeps.
Trust in the Lord, and you will be kept safe.
Amen.

ISAIAH 6

Choral or Congregational Call to Prayer

"Holy, Holy, Holy! Lord God Almighty," by Reginald Heber (st. 3)

Invitation

Let us stand amazed in the presence of the One
who is closer to us than we are to ourselves.
☩ *Silence*

Prayer of Confession

Gracious God,
 you are always present,
 always near,
  and yet at times we do not see you in the temple;
  we do not know that we are standing
   on holy ground.
Gracious God,
 you often speak to us,
 even calling us by name,
  and yet we cannot discern your voice.
Forgive our distracted minds and hardened hearts,
 through Jesus Christ, our Lord . . .
☩ *Silence*

Words of Assurance

Brothers and sisters, believe the good news:
Seek first the kingdom of God,
 and God's righteousness,
 and all these things will be given to you. Amen.

EZEKIEL 1

Choral or Congregational Call to Prayer

"Immortal, Invisible, God Only Wise," by Walter Chalmers Smith (st. 2)

Invitation

Let us enter into the mystery of the One who is
    our creator, our redeemer, and our sustainer.
✝ *Silence*

Prayer of Confession

God of abundance,
    in our poverty we see only a glimpse
    of your providence.
Amid the noises that bombard us
    we fail to hear your words of blessing.
Across the silences that separate us
    we miss your gifts of mercy and healing.
Draw near to us.
Open our hearts, our minds, and our doors
    to those who speak to us on your behalf,
    not only today and now in this holy place,
    but in all places and in all the days to come.
Speak Lord.
We are listening . . .
✝ *Silence*

Words of Assurance

Leader: God's light pierces the darkness of our sin,
    and our lives are flooded with light.
God's word pierces the silence of our world,
    and our hearts are filled with grace.
Receive the good news of Jesus Christ,
    light of the world,
    the word become flesh.
In his name, your sins are forgiven!
People: In his name, your sins are forgiven!

MICAH 6

Choral or Congregational Call to Prayer

"What Does the Lord Require of You?" by Jim Strathdee

Invitation

The Lord's voice is clear, compassionate, and just.
Let us listen with all our hearts and with all our minds.
✟ *Silence*

Prayer of Confession

O God, we want to know what is required of us,
   and yet we are sometimes
      fearful of giving ourselves to you.
We sense a call to reach out toward others,
   and yet we often look upon the needy
      with more judgment than mercy.
When we have not heard the cries of the needy
   or noticed the bruised and broken people along our paths,
Forgive us.
Grant us an integrated life
   of devotion and service;
   profession and practice;
   holiness and compassion;
   through Jesus Christ, our Savior.
✟ *Silence*

Words of Assurance

Return to the Lord
   with all your heart
   and you will be healed.
Trust in the Lord
   with all your heart
   and you will be redeemed.
In the name of Jesus Christ, you are forgiven.
Glory to God! Amen.

MATTHEW 4; LUKE 4

Choral or Congregational Call to Prayer

"Lord, Who Throughout These Forty Days," by Claudia F. Hernaman (st. 1)

Invitation

Let us draw near to God
and receive holy comfort in our times of testing.
✟ *Silence*

Prayer of Confession

Almighty God, your blessed Son was led by the Spirit
to be tempted by Satan.
We ask for your help
as we are assaulted by temptations.
We confess our weakness in the face of testing,
and our lack of courage.
We acknowledge our dependence upon you.
Keep before us the example of Jesus,
who listened for your voice,
remembered your word,
and overcame temptation.
As we are conformed to his life,
may we also be transformed by his death
in the gift of his body, broken for us,
and his blood, poured out for us,
a sign of our forgiveness.
✟ *Silence*

Words of Assurance

We have not a high priest
who cannot sympathize with our weaknesses,
but one who, tempted as we are, is yet without sin.
In the name of Jesus Christ, our mediator,
we are forgiven. Amen.

MATTHEW 5

Choral or Congregational Call to Prayer

"For the Fruits of This Creation," by Fred Pratt Green (st. 1)

Invitation

Let us offer the gift that God most desires:
a humble spirit and a contrite heart.
Let us kneel before the One who creates,
calls, and comforts us.

✟ *Silence*

Prayer of Confession

O God of life, love, and light,
you call us to be stewards of your gifts;
instruments of your peace;
witnesses to your glory.
Where we bury our talents in the ground,
forgive us.
Where we construct walls instead of bridges,
forgive us.
Where we hide your light under a basket,
forgive us.
Lead us, in your righteousness,
from darkness to light;
from hatred to love;
from death to life.

✟ *Silence*

Words of Assurance

O God, who spoke all creation into being
and called it good,
You are always reaching out to restore creation
into your image, which is love.
Through your Son Jesus Christ,
in his infinite mercy,
and by the power of his cross,
we are forgiven. Amen.

MATTHEW 6

Choral or Congregational Call to Prayer:
"Great Is Thy Faithfulness," by Thomas O. Chisholm (st. 1)

Invitation
Let us draw near to the One
      who is our help and our salvation.
✞ *Silence*

Prayer of Confession
O God,
    you are always giving to us out of your abundance,
    but our hands are too full to receive your blessings.
You are always fulfilling your promise
    to provide for us in the present,
    but our minds are anxious about the future.
You are always willing to hear our confession,
    but our hearts are hardened to your grace.
O God of loaves and fishes,
    meet the hungers of your people,
    and strengthen us in body, mind, and spirit.
In the name of Jesus Christ, we pray . . .
✞ *Silence*

Words of Assurance
God is the giver of every good and perfect gift.
In the name of Jesus Christ,
God's great gift to the world,
    we are forgiven.
Thanks be to God! Amen.

LUKE 15

Choral or Congregational Call to Prayer
"Surely the Presence of the Lord," by Lanny Wolfe

Invitation
Let us seek the Lord while he may be found;
let us call upon the Lord while he is near.
☦ *Silence*

Prayer of Confession
O God, we seek you because you have first sought us;
we love you because you have first loved us.
We pray to you,
not because of our worthiness, but at your invitation.
Hear the cries of our hearts,
and mend the brokenness of our lives.
Draw near to us,
that the distance that separates us
might be bridged by grace,
which is your great gift to us,
through Jesus Christ our Savior. Amen.
☦ *Silence*

Words of Assurance
While the child was a long way off,
You ran and embraced the wayward child and said,
"You were lost, but now you are found."
The angels rejoice in the return of even one sinner
who repents.
Thanks be to God!
Amen.

JOHN 6

Choral or Congregational Call to Prayer

"You Satisfy the Hungry Heart," by Omer Westendorf (st. 3)

Invitation

At the invitation of Jesus Christ,
    let us come into God's presence.
The Lord is our host,
    and we are guests.
✟ *Silence*

Prayer of Confession

O God,
    you have invited us to feast at your table,
    and we have rejected your invitation.
You have called us to taste your goodness,
    and we have turned away to other gods.
You have commanded us to share your bounty with others,
    and we have consumed at the expense of our neighbors.
For those of us who are hungry,
O God, give bread.
And for those of us who have bread,
    give us a hunger for justice and righteousness.
Through Jesus Christ,
    the bread of life,
we pray.
✟ *Silence*

Words of Assurance

New every morning are the mercies of God;
    great is your faithfulness.
For the provision of every need,
    and for the forgiveness of sin,
    we give you thanks and praise. Amen.

ACTS 2
Choral or Congregational Call to Prayer
"Breathe on Me, Breath of God," by Edwin Hatch (st. 1)
Invitation
Let us open our hearts and our minds
    to the movement of the Spirit!
God is here!
✞ *Silence*

Prayer of Confession

O God,
    your Spirit moves among us,
    calling us to peace.
We confess our anxiety.
Your Spirit moves among us,
    calling us to mission.
We confess our passivity.
Your Spirit moves among us,
    calling us to bear witness.
We confess our silence.
Your Spirit moves among us,
    calling us to unity.
We confess our divisions.
Spirit of the living God,
    be present with wind, word, and fire.
Holy Spirit,
    rest upon us, and dwell within us.
✞ *Silence*

Words of Assurance

"In the days to come," says the Lord,
"I will pour out my spirit on all flesh."
Sisters and brothers, believe the good news:
God is with us!
Thanks be to God. Amen.

ROMANS 6

Choral or Congregational Call to Prayer

"Just as I Am, Without One Plea," by Charlotte Elliott
(st. 5)

Invitation

We come into the presence of the Lord
   not by our own merits,
   but through gracious invitation.
Let us confess our sin before God.
✠ *Silence*

Prayer of Confession

O God,
   you seem so far away.
We want to act in ways that are right,
   but we find ourselves doing just the opposite.
You are holy and we are flawed.
You are strong and we are weak.
You are merciful and we are unforgiving.
Remove the sin that separates us from you;
   gather us into the arms of your mercy;
   and heal us through the One who is crucified and risen,
Jesus Christ our Lord.
✠ *Silence*

Words of Assurance

If we have died with Christ,
   we shall also be raised with him.
If we confess our sin,
   we are set free from the law
   and offered the free gift of grace.
In the name of Jesus Christ,
   we are forgiven.
Amen.

1 CORINTHIANS 11

Choral or Congregational Call to Prayer

"One Bread, One Body," by John B. Foley (st. 3)

Invitation

God prepares a table for us;
God welcomes us at a great banquet;
God provides all that we need.
✝ *Silence*

Prayer of Confession

O God, you are present in our midst,
    and yet our eyes do not see you.
You speak through word, you sing through the psalms,
    and yet our ears do not hear you.
You feed us at the Lord's Table,
    and yet we are hungry.
You touch us through the body of Christ,
    and we sense that we are alone.
Be present at our table, Lord,
    and be present to us in our neighbor.
In the name of Jesus Christ, we pray.
✝ *Silence*

Words of Assurance

Hear the good news of the gospel:
Jesus says, "I have come that you may have life,
    and have it in abundance."
His broken body and his shed blood
    are the signs of our reconciliation.
Thanks be to God! Amen.

1 CORINTHIANS 13

Choral or Congregational Call to Prayer

"The Gift of Love," by Hal Hopson (st. 1)

Invitation

God is love, and God invites us into his loving presence.
☦ *Silence*

Prayer of Confession

O God,
    you are the source of life, light, and love.
We pause to confess our human condition:
    we have preferred death to life;
        darkness to light;
        hatred to love.
And yet we also profess with boldness
    the good news of our faith:
    that you see us as we really are;
    that you are always transforming us;
        always healing us;
        always saving us.
Create us anew, O Lord;
    fill us with your Holy Spirit,
    and lead us in paths of righteousness.
☦ *Silence*

Words of Assurance (adapted from John 3:16-17)

For God so loved the world
    that he gave his only Son,
    so that everyone who believes in him
    may not perish
        but have eternal life.
Indeed, God sent his Son into the world
    not to condemn the world,
    but in order that the world might be saved through him.

2 CORINTHIANS 5

Choral or Congregational Call to Prayer

"Joyful, Joyful, We Adore Thee," by Henry Van Dyke (st. 1)

Invitation

Let us dwell not in the past,
    nor in the future,
but let us consider the presence of Almighty God
    in our midst,
    in this moment.
Let us draw near, by faith.
Let us be silent.

✟ *Silence*

Prayer of Confession

O God,
    we sometimes dwell more in the past
    than in the present or the future.
We sometimes doubt that you are alive;
    that you are real;
    that you matter.
We look at each day as more of the same
    and wonder if there is anything new under the sun.
Forgive us for our lack of faith in your unseen power.
Have mercy upon us when our love for you wanes.
Grant us hope in the future
    that you plan and prepare for us.

✟ *Silence*

Words of Assurance

If anyone is in Christ,
    there is a new creation.
The old has passed away;
    behold, all things are new.
All this is the gracious work of God in us,
    through us, and for us. Amen.

2 CORINTHIANS 12

Choral or Congregational Call to Prayer

"Precious Lord, Take My Hand," by Thomas A. Dorsey (st. 1)

Invitation

Let us draw near to God, whose strength is made manifest
in our weakness.

✟ *Silence*

Prayer of Confession

O God,
    we profess a faith that we do not always live.
We hope for a future that we cannot always see.
We express love,
    but we attach limits and conditions.
Move us toward a full acceptance of your gifts—
    faith, hope, and love.
Give us hearts to know you.
Give us eyes to see you.
Give us hands to serve you.
In the name of Jesus, we pray.

✟ *Silence*

Words of Assurance

Leader: Brothers and sisters,
    this is love:
not that we love God,
    but that God first loved us
    and gave his Son to be the sacrifice for our sins.
In the name of Jesus Christ,
    and through trust in his loving presence,
    you are forgiven.
**People: In the name of Jesus Christ,
    and through trust in his loving presence,
    you are forgiven.
All: Amen.**

EPHESIANS 3

Choral or Congregational Call to Prayer

"Blest Be the Tie That Binds," by John Fawcett (st. 1)

Invitation

Let us unite in prayer, in the common language
    of dependence upon the source of life and health.
☩ *Silence*

Prayer of Confession

In you, O God,
    every family on earth receives its name.
As we consider the divisions that scar our nations,
    our communities, and our families,
we pray for illumination, that our homes will be infused
    with the light of your love.
Where we have not reached out with compassion
    toward those who are lonely,
        awaken us.
Where we have not responded with courage
    on behalf of those who are in danger,
        forgive us.
Where we have not shared in the burdens or bonds
    of family life,
        have mercy upon us.
Remind us that we love because you first loved us.
Grant us your peace, through Jesus Christ our Lord.
☩ *Silence*

Words of Assurance

We are your beloved children, O God,
    and you are our loving parent.
Your grace overcomes our guilt.
Your power overcomes our resistance.
Your love overcomes our sin.
Thanks be to God! Amen.

PHILIPPIANS 1

Choral or Congregational Call to Prayer

"I Want to Walk as a Child of the Light," by Kathleen Thomerson (st. 3)

Invitation

Let us behold the coming of the Lord.
☦ *Silence*

Prayer of Confession

O God, you have begun a good work in us,
    and you are faithful to complete it.
And yet our pessimism about what *is*
    often overwhelms our optimism about what is to come.
Open our hearts,
    that we might trust in your gracious providence.
Open our minds,
    that we might believe in your mighty power.
Open our eyes,
    that we might see the coming kingdom,
        for which we pray.
Forgive us for failures of imagination, vision, and hope.
Increase our faith.
☦ *Silence*

Words of Assurance

God is gracious and merciful,
    slow to anger, and abounding in steadfast love.
In the name of Jesus Christ,
    our sins are forgiven.
Thanks be to God!
Amen.

CHAPTER FOUR

CONFESSION, ASSURANCE, AND THE LITURGICAL YEAR

ADVENT

Choral or Congregational Call to Prayer

"Come, Thou Long-expected Jesus," by Charles Wesley (st. 1)

Invitation

Prepare the way of the Lord. Make a straight path for him.
✟ Silence

Prayer of Confession

We confess to you, O God,
  that we inhabit the ruined cities,
    where trust has been shaken;
    where dreams have become dim memories;
    where hopes have turned to despair.
We have learned to be at home in a broken world.
We have pursued happiness and pleasure
  rather than peace and joy.

And yet your faithfulness sustains us and revives us,
and your promise raises us into a new life.
Forgive us, we pray.
Restore to us the joy of your salvation,
through the Savior, Jesus Christ.
☩ *Silence*

Words of Assurance

God says,
"I am creating a new heaven and a new earth."
Behold the works of the Lord.
In Jesus Christ, all things have been made new.
Amen.

ADVENT

Choral or Congregational Call to Prayer

"Come, Thou Long-expected Jesus," by Charles Wesley (st. 2)

Invitation

The Lord is surely coming.
Let every heart prepare him room.
☩ *Silence*

Prayer of Confession

O God,
the journey through this season can be exhausting,
stressful, and confusing.
At times hope eludes us,
peace is out of the question,
and joy seems impossible.
We confess our need for your coming, once again.
Open our eyes and ears
so that we might see the glory of the Lord
and hear the voices of angels.
Strengthen our hands and hearts
so that we might share your love,
for the sake of the world you seek to save,
through Jesus Christ.
☩ *Silence*

Words of Assurance

"The days are surely coming," says the Lord,
"when I will pour out my spirit on all flesh."
"The days are surely coming," says the Lord,
"when I will make a new covenant with them."
The time is fulfilled and the kingdom is at hand.
Brothers and sisters, believe the good news:
Messiah is coming!

73

ADVENT

Choral or Congregational Call to Prayer

"O Come, O Come, Emmanuel," 9th cent. Latin; trans. by Henry Sloane Coffin and Laurence Hull Stookey (st. 1)

Invitation

Our Savior draws near: Let every heart prepare him room.
☦ *Silence*

Prayer of Confession

O God, we look beyond ourselves,
    upon a world of false hopes and broken promises,
    and we are prone to lower our expectations.
We look within ourselves,
    upon mixed motives and wounded hearts,
    and we are inclined to despair.
And yet the good news is sure
    and worthy of full acceptance:
        your promise will be fulfilled;
        your covenant is everlasting;
        your words will not pass away.
Draw near to us;
    fill us with hope;
    remind us that the day of the Lord is surely coming.
☦ *Silence*

Words of Assurance

Hear the good news:
God the Father has come near to us,
    in Jesus Christ, our Savior,
    through the presence and power of the Holy Spirit.
Amen.

CHRISTMAS

Choral or Congregational Call to Prayer
"O Little Town of Bethlehem," by Phillips Brooks (st. 3)

Invitation
Let every heart prepare him room.
O come, let us adore him.
✟ *Silence*

Prayer of Confession
O God,
 the darkness of the world surrounds us and,
  if we are honest,
we confess that the darkness of the world resides within us.
At times, we prefer the darkness to the light.
Have mercy upon us
 according to your steadfast love and infinite mercy.
Remind us that the light shines in the darkness,
 and the darkness has not overcome it.
Guide our feet in paths of righteousness
 and teach us to walk in the light,
  through Jesus Christ our Savior.
✟ *Silence*

Words of Assurance
The word became flesh and lived among us,
 full of grace and truth.
O God,
 come to us;
 abide with us,
Emmanuel,
 to save us;
 to set us free. Amen.

EPIPHANY

Choral or Congregational Call to Prayer

"We Three Kings of Orient Are," by John H. Hopkins Jr. (st. 1)

Invitation

Let us journey to the place
   where the Christ child awaits us,
   where the light of God shines brightly.
☩ *Silence*

Prayer of Confession

O God,
by the leading of a star
   your only Son was made known to us.
And yet we confess that we have preferred darkness
   to light;
our own plans and purposes
   to your guidance and direction;
our own pride and will
   to your power and glory.
Forgive us, Lord.
Grant us wisdom to behold the radiance
   that shines upon us
   and grace to walk in the light of your love.
☩ *Silence*

Words of Assurance

You guide us into life, light, and love,
God of wonder.
You invite us to experience new birth.
May the glory of Jesus Christ
   shine in the darkest places of our lives,
   and may we receive the gift of salvation
   that is your desire for us. Amen.

BAPTISM OF THE LORD
(OR BAPTISMAL RENEWAL)

Choral or Congregational Call to Prayer

"Shall We Gather at the River?" by Robert Lowry (st. 1)

Invitation

Let us draw near to receive the living waters
of Jesus' presence.
✝ *Silence*

Prayer of Confession

O Lord, we gather as unclean people.
Our motives are not always pure.
Our desires are not always appropriate.
Our lives are not always ordered.
Our actions are not always constructive.
Remind us that we have been baptized;
that you have created us,
called us by name,
taken us by the hand,
and blessed us as your beloved children.
Through the presence of your Holy Spirit,
free us from all that is past,
and empower us for all that awaits us in the future;
through Jesus Christ, we pray.
✝ *Silence*

Words of Assurance

Let the healing stream of God's love
wash over you.
Let the indwelling waters of Jesus
quench your thirst.
Let the river of life, the renewing Spirit,
guide you into all truth.
Amen.

TRANSFIGURATION

Choral or Congregational Call to Prayer

"Christ Is the World's Light," by Fred Pratt Green (st. 1)

Invitation

Let us open our hearts and minds
to receive the light that is coming into the world.
✞ *Silence*

Prayer of Confession

O God of glory and mercy,
  you reveal yourself to us in Jesus.
And yet at times our eyes do not see him;
  our minds do not know him;
  our hearts do not love him;
  our voices do not praise him.
Be thou our vision, O Lord;
  expand our perception,
  increase our comprehension,
  strengthen our passion,
  and transform us through acts of worship and
    service.
In the name of the One whose light shines in the darkness,
  even Jesus Christ our Lord.
✞ *Silence*

Words of Assurance

God is light,
  and in him is no darkness.
If we confess our sin,
God is faithful and just
  to forgive our sin
  and to cleanse us from all unrighteousness. Amen.

ASH WEDNESDAY

Choral or Congregational Call to Prayer
"Pass Me Not, O Gentle Savior," by Fanny J. Crosby (st. 3)

Invitation
Let us humble ourselves so that God might be exalted.
Let us turn away self and repent of our sin.
✟ *Silence*

Prayer of Confession
O God,
  because we did not create ourselves,
  because we do not save ourselves,
  because we cannot sustain ourselves,
We come aware of our poverty and your riches.
We come confessing our limitations,
  alongside your infinite strength and goodness.
We acknowledge the evil that we have done
  and the good that we have left undone,
  the pride that pushes you away,
  the envy that desires what belongs to others,
  and the greed that consumes us
    and all that surrounds us.
We pray for open hearts,
  that we might receive your gifts,
and open minds,
  that we might know your truth.
✟ *Silence*

Words of Assurance
Leader: "In returning and rest, you will be saved,"
  says the Lord.
In quietness and trust, we find strength.
In the midst of death, there is resurrection and new life.
In the name of Jesus Christ,
  you are forgiven.
People: In the name of Jesus Christ, you are forgiven.

LENT

Choral or Congregational Call to Prayer

"*Pues Si Vivmos* (When We Are Living)," by Anonymous (st.1), trans. by Elise S. Eslinger (st. 1)

Invitation

The mercies of the Lord are from everlasting to everlasting.
☥ *Silence*

Prayer of Confession

Our temptations, O Lord,
    are the very tests that came to you—
    to be relevant; to be powerful; to be spectacular.
We may not be asked to turn stones into bread
    or to be in control of vast kingdoms
    or to throw ourselves down from a tall spire,
and yet, your temptations are the very ones that we face.
Where we have listened to other voices,
    forgive us.
Where we have sought the applause of others,
    forgive us.
Where we have worshiped other gods,
    forgive us.
Give us purity of heart and clarity of vision.
Help us hear your voice
    to seek your kingdom and its righteousness,
    to worship you alone.
In the name of the One who was tested
    in every respect as we are, and yet knew no sin,
    even Jesus Christ our Savior. Amen.
☥ *Silence*

Words of Assurance

We thank you, O God, for the good news
    that we may approach the throne of grace with boldness
    so that we may receive mercy and find grace
        to help in time of need. Amen.

LENT

Choral or Congregational Call to Prayer

"Beneath the Cross of Jesus," by Elizabeth C. Clephane (st. 3)

Invitation

"Come, let us reason together," says the Lord.
✝ *Silence*

Prayer of Confession

O God, I am strong;
   at least I think I am strong.
I like to be in control.
I like to be at the center.
Maybe being strong is about survival;
   about perseverance;
   about doing what I ought to do.
But at times I am aware that I am not so strong.
At times I sense that I am not in control.
At times I know that I am not centered in you,
   but in myself.
Strip away the illusion of strength,
   and in my weakness help me live by faith.
Take away the illusion of control,
   and in my uncertainty lead me to live by hope.
Remove the illusion that I am at the center of all things,
   and, even in my pride, guide me to a life of love.
You are the vine and I am the branch.
Apart from you I can do nothing.
✝ *Silence*

Words of Assurance

Those who wait on the Lord shall renew their strength.
They shall mount up with wings as eagles.
They shall run and not be weary.
They shall walk and not faint. Amen.

PALM/PASSION SUNDAY

Choral or Congregational Call to Prayer
"Beneath the Cross of Jesus," by Elizabeth C. Clephane (st. 1)

Invitation
Let us go the garden of Gethsemane,
where Jesus prays with and for us.
✟ *Silence*

Prayer of Confession
Lord Jesus,
We want to be your followers,
    and yet we hesitate to take up the cross.
We want to be glorified with you,
    and yet we recoil from the shame that you endure.
We want to enjoy the abundant life that you offer,
    and yet we fear the loss of life that you require.
Look upon us with compassion
    in the days ahead,
And unite us,
    not only in the fellowship of your suffering,
    but also in the power of your resurrection.
✟ *Silence*

Words of Assurance
God shows his love for us in that
    while we were yet sinners
    Christ died for us.
Through the power of the crucified Lord,
    we are redeemed.
Thanks be to God!
Amen.

MAUNDY THURSDAY

Choral or Congregational Call to Prayer

"Let All Mortal Flesh Keep Silence," Liturgy of Saint James, 4th cent., trans. by Gerard Moultrie (st. 3)

Invitation

Let us be still. Let us keep silence.
Let us prepare ourselves for this holy evening.
✟ *Silence*

Prayer of Confession

O God, you come to seek and save us,
    and yet we resist your coming.
We want to determine the conditions of love.
We want to place limits on love.
And so we keep you at a distance,
    rejecting the bread of Christ;
    fearing the touch of the master's hand;
    dreading the process of healing;
    questioning the possibility of reconciliation.
We are threatened by the intimacy of a love
    that sees us as we really are and not as we pretend to be.
We are overwhelmed by a love
    that comes to us as pure gift and not as our achievement
    or right.
Break down the barriers that separate us.
Remind us that you love us.
✟ *Silence*

Words of Assurance

Leader: Brothers and sisters, God is love.
And if God loves us, we also ought to love one another.
In the name of Jesus Christ,
Who loved us and gave himself for us, you are forgiven.
People: In the name of Jesus Christ,
    who loved us and gave himself for us, we are forgiven.
All: Thanks be to God!

GOOD FRIDAY

Choral or Congregational Call to Prayer

"Jesus, Remember Me," from Luke 23:42 (sing twice)

Invitation

Behold, the Lamb of God,
    who takes away the sin of the world.
Let us consider the mercies of God.
☦ *Silence*

Prayer of Confession

Lord Jesus Christ,
    you became weak so that we might be strong;
    you poured yourself out so that we might be filled;
    your body was broken so that we might be fed;
    you died upon a cross so that we might live.
And yet your ways are not our ways.
Save us from our strengths.
Place within us a hunger for righteousness
    and a thirst for justice.
Remind us that in giving we receive.
Keep us near the cross,
    a sign of judgment and hope,
    of forgiveness and new life.
☦ *Silence*

Words of Assurance

The cross is foolishness to those who are perishing,
But to those who are being saved
It is the power and wisdom of God.
In the name of the crucified Lord, Jesus Christ,
We pass from death to life.
Thanks be to God!

EASTER

Choral or Congregational Call to Prayer

"Hymn of Promise," by Natalie Sleeth (st. 3)

Invitation

Let us watch for the dawn of new light.
Let us listen for the whispers of new insight.
Let us wait for the Lord.
✟ *Silence*

Prayer of Confession

O God, on this holy morning
    we acknowledge the inadequacy of our resurrection faith.
Where we have not perceived
    the breaking forth of your light,
        forgive us.
Where we have been slow to believe
    the promises of your prophets,
        have mercy upon us.
Where we have viewed one another
    from a human point of view,
        grant us the peace of our risen Lord,
Jesus Christ.
✟ *Silence*

Words of Assurance

Love's redeeming work is done.
Christ is risen
    and has conquered sin and death.
By the gracious gift of resurrection,
    all things are made new.
Alleluia!

SUNDAY AFTER EASTER

Choral or Congregational Call to Prayer

"Thine Be the Glory," by Edmond L. Budry; trans. by R. Birch Hoyle

Invitation

Our hope is in the Lord.
Let us draw near,
   by faith,
   in expectation and prayer.
✿ *Silence*

Prayer of Confession

O God of new beginnings,
   you teach us to pray for the inbreaking of your Spirit,
   and yet we acknowledge a level of comfort
      with the status quo.
O God of new creation,
   you invite us to pray for the coming of your kingdom,
   and yet we confess a stubbornness
      about our own sense of direction.
O God of empty tomb, crown, and cross,
   you disrupt the patterns of our everyday lies,
   and yet at times we are resistant to change.
Break our hearts of stone
   with your words of healing and hope, risen Lord.
Forgive us,
   and walk with us into a new future.
✿ *Silence*

Words of Assurance

The risen Lord walks before you
   to give you hope,
and beside you
   to give you strength.
The risen Lord dwells within you
   to give you peace. Amen.

86

ASCENSION SUNDAY

Choral or Congregational Call to Prayer

"Fairest Lord Jesus," by *Münster Gesanbuch*; trans. Joseph August Seiss (st. 4)

Invitation

Let us confess our dependence upon the risen Lord,
  who is risen, has ascended,
  and is seated at the right hand of God.
✞ *Silence*

Prayer of Confession

O God of promise and fulfillment,
  you command us to pray for the coming of your Spirit,
  and yet we confess our reluctance to watch and wait.
O God of power and might,
  you invite us to pray for the coming of your kingdom,
  and yet we acknowledge our unwillingness
    to witness and work.
O God of cross and crown, wind and fire,
  you reveal yourself to us
  in ordinary and extravagant ways,
and yet at times we do not perceive your presence,
  hear your voice, receive your blessing,
  or share your love with others.
Forgive us, in the name of the One
  who is seated at your right hand,
  even Jesus Christ our Lord.
✞ *Silence*

Words of Assurance

May God grant us a spirit of wisdom
  so that we might know
  the immeasurable greatness of God's power.
Jesus said, "I will not leave you comfortless,
  but I will send the Holy Spirit to comfort you,
  to encourage you, and to give you peace." Amen.

PENTECOST

Choral or Congregational Call to Prayer

"Spirit of the Living God," by Daniel Iverson (sing twice)

Invitation

Give us ears to hear
what you are saying to the church, O God.
✟ *Silence*

Prayer of Confession

O God, your Spirit moves among us, calling us to peace.
    We confess our anxiety.
Your Spirit moves among us, calling us to mission.
    We confess our passivity.
Your Spirit moves among us, calling us to bear witness.
    We confess our silence.
Your Spirit moves among us, calling us to unity.
    We confess our divisions.
Spirit of the living God,
    be present with wind, word, and fire.
Holy Spirit, rest upon us and dwell within us.
✟ *Silence*

Words of Assurance

"The days are coming," says the Lord,
    "when I will pour out my spirit on all flesh."
On that day, everyone who calls upon the name of the Lord
    will be saved.
Giver of life and author of salvation,
    you are present in this moment in peace and power.
Come, Holy Spirit!

TRINITY SUNDAY

Choral or Congregational Call to Prayer

"Come, Thou Almighty King," by Anonymous

Invitation

Let us come into the presence of God the Father,
  through Jesus Christ the Son,
  in the power of the Holy Spirit.
✟ *Silence*

Prayer of Confession

O God, you are One,
  and yet within your very life
  you are also relationship and community.
Where we seek to live apart from your presence and power,
    forgive us.
Where we distance ourselves from others,
    have mercy upon us.
Where we suffer the pain of division,
    grant us the gift of your peace.
Holy and Triune God,
  in your mercy,
  hear our prayers.
✟ *Silence*

Words of Assurance

Trust in the assurance that the One who creates you,
  the One who redeems you,
  and the One who sustains you
  is Love.
Believe the good news: God is with us.
Thanks be to God!

SUNDAY AFTER PENTECOST

Choral or Congregational Call to Prayer

"Spirit Song," by John Wimber (st. 1)

Invitation

Let us draw near to the God whose grace surrounds us.

✝ *Silence*

Prayer of Confession

Gracious God,
   you love us in ways that are
      beyond our comprehension,
   and yet we are at times distant,
      distracted, and discouraged.
We have lost our sense of connection with you.
We come into your presence after absences
   that leave us confused, exhausted, and alone.
We ask for the indwelling of your Holy Spirit.
We cry out for your real presence in our lives,
   in the name of Jesus Christ, our Savior.

✝ *Silence*

Words of Assurance

Brothers and sisters,
   the mercies of God are from everlasting to everlasting.
In the name of Jesus Christ,
   receive the grace of God
   that is beyond our efforts and in spite of our failures.
The goodness of God is amazing.
The gift of God is the forgiveness of our sin
   and the promise of new life.
Thanks be to God. Amen.

˙SUNDAY AFTER PENTECOST

Choral or Congregational Call to Prayer

"Holy Spirit, Come, Confirm Us," by Brian Foley (st. 1)

Invitation

The fresh winds of the Spirit are stirring among us.
Let us be attentive to the movement of the Spirit.
☫ *Silence*

Prayer of Confession

O God,
    our very present help,
your Son Jesus returned to you and sent the comforter,
    the Spirit of truth,
        to be with us.
Have mercy on us
    in our estrangement,
    for there is distance between us.
Draw near to us
    and place us in the shadow of your wings,
    where there is life and joy and peace.
In the name of Jesus Christ, we pray.
☫ *Silence*

Words of Assurance

Leader: "I will not leave you comfortless," says the Lord,
"I am coming to you.
    I will place my Spirit within you,
        and you will live."
In the name of Jesus Christ,
    who promises to be with us always,
    you are forgiven.
**People: In the name of Jesus Christ,
    who promises to be with us always,
    we are forgiven.
All: Amen.**

91

ORDINARY TIME

Choral or Congregational Call to Prayer

"Praise God, from Whom All Blessings Flow," by Thomas Ken

Invitation

We live in God's world.
Let us with humility listen for the word of the Lord.
✟ *Silence*

Prayer of Confession

Father, Son, and Holy Spirit,
    you have created a world
    filled with awe and abundance,
    and yet we live in the midst of boredom and scarcity.
Forgive us.
Father, Son, and Holy Spirit,
    you have entered into our world with grace and truth,
    and yet we live in the midst of judgment and deception.
Have mercy upon us.
Father, Son, and Holy Spirit,
    you have touched our world with power and presence,
    and yet we live in the midst of despair and loneliness.
Grant us your peace.
✟ *Silence*

Words of Assurance

The whole earth is filled with your glory, O God.
Your love is broader than our imagining,
    and your grace is beyond our comprehension.
You love us so much you sent your only Son
    into this world to be our Savior.
Thanks be to God!

ORDINARY TIME

Choral or Congregational Call to Prayer

"Love Divine, All Loves Excelling," by Charles Wesley (st. 2)

Invitation

Come, Holy Spirit, fill the hearts of your faithful,
and kindle in us the fire of your love.
✟ *Silence*

Prayer of Confession

Almighty and merciful God,
  our lives are your good creation,
  and yet we confess that we are sometimes
  out of harmony with your intention.
We are overcommitted and anxious,
  inactive and perplexed.
Forgive us.
Lord Jesus,
  we possess neither the clarity of mind
  nor the energy of will to make a difference
    in this world,
  and yet we yearn for a sense of purpose and direction.
Have mercy on us.
Spirit of God,
  descend upon our hearts;
  give life to your body, the church;
  and renew the face of the earth.
✟ *Silence*

Words of Assurance

We boast not in our goodness,
  but in the gift of God,
  which is salvation through Jesus Christ.
For this greatest gift,
We give our thanks and praise to God. Amen.

WORLD COMMUNION

Choral or Congregational Call to Prayer
"Become to Us the Living Bread," by Miriam Drury (st. 3)

Invitation
Let us make room in our hearts
for the wideness of God's mercy,
which extends to us and to all people.
✞ *Silence*

Prayer of Confession
We come as sinners to the gospel feast, O God.
And yet we come with hesitation and ambivalence.
If we have rejected your invitation,
forgive us.
If we have resisted your embrace,
have mercy on us.
If we have wandered from your purpose,
grant us your peace.
Your greatest desire is that we taste
the riches of your grace.
Draw us into a deeper communion with you
and with your people across this planet.
✞ *Silence*

Words of Assurance
As you broke the bread
and fed the multitudes,
Your riches extend to every hungry heart, Lord Jesus.
Nourish us.
Sustain us.
Become the living bread that gives life to us. Amen.

ALL SAINTS

Choral or Congregational Call to Prayer
"For All the Saints," by William W. How (st. 4)

Invitation
Grace and peace to all the saints.
Let us confess our sins with all who love the Lord.
✞ *Silence*

Prayer of Confession
We confess our inclination, O God,
    to sense that we are alone in the faith.
We neglect the history of those
    who have gone before us;
    we take for granted their perseverance;
        we have lost touch with the wisdom
            that would lead us to life.
Have mercy upon us, O Lord.
Call to mind our mothers and fathers in the faith,
    who ran the race before us,
and let us draw strength
        from their examples.
✞ *Silence*

Words of Assurance
God has not given us a spirit of fear,
    but of love and power
        and self-discipline.
Let us remember the goodness
    of God in the lives of the saints,
and let us draw strength
    from the cloud of witnesses
        that surrounds us.
Thanks be to God!

CHRIST THE KING

Choral or Congregational Call to Prayer

"Soon and Very Soon," by Andraé Crouch (st. 1)

Invitation

Jesus is the beginning and the end,
The first and the last,
    and is seated at the right hand of God.
Let us humble ourselves,
So that he might be exalted.
✟ *Silence*

Prayer of Confession

O God, the coming of your kingdom
    calls forth our repentance.
Forgive us.
The power that comes from on high
    stoops to our weakness.
Have mercy upon us.
The glory of your name
    rises above our ambition.
Grant us your peace.
Order our lives before you, Living God,
    that the kingdoms of the world
    may become the kingdoms of our Lord
    and of his Christ.
✟ *Silence*

Words of Assurance

At the name of Jesus Christ,
    every knee will bow and every tongue confess
    that Jesus Christ is Lord,
    to the glory of God the Father.
Let us take comfort in the power of Almighty God
    to forgive our sins
    and to cleanse us from all unrighteousness.

Resources

(For further study and reflection)

De Waal, Esther. *Living with Contradiction*. San Francisco: HarperSanFrancisco, 1989.

Dunnam, Maxie, and Kimberly Dunnam Reisman. *The Workbook on the Seven Deadly Sins*. Nashville: Upper Room Books, 1997.

Jones, L. Gregory. *Embodying Forgiveness: A Theological Analysis*. Grand Rapids: Eerdmans, 1995.

Lewis. C. S. *Mere Christianity*. San Francisco: HarperCollins, 2001.

———. *The Screwtape Letters*. New York: Simon & Schuster, 1961.

Niebuhr, Reinhold. *Moral Man and Immoral Society*. New York: Scribner, 1932.

O'Connor, Flannery. *The Complete Stories*. New York: Farrar, Straus and Giroux, 1972.

Patton, John. *Is Human Forgiveness Possible?* Nashville: Abingdon Press, 1985.

Taylor, Barbara Brown. *Speaking of Sin*. Cambridge: Cowley, 2000.

Wink, Walter. *Engaging the Powers*. Minneapolis: Fortress Press, 1992.

Yancey, Philip. *What's So Amazing about Grace?* Grand Rapids: Zondervan, 1997.

SCRIPTURE INDEX

Scripture Index

Hymn Index